Simple e

Earning money online

Chapter 1: Introduction

In today's digital era, the internet has gained immense importance and offers us numerous opportunities to supplement our income comfortably from home. Whether you're looking for an additional income stream, wanting to give your current career a boost, or simply aiming for financial freedom, earning money online can be an incredibly exciting and rewarding option.

In this book, we will delve into the various strategies, platforms, and methods that can help you effortlessly earn money online. It's important to me that the explanations are understandable and easy to implement. My goal is to provide you with the necessary knowledge to understand and successfully apply the different ways of making money online.

You'll be surprised by how diverse the options are for earning money online. From affiliate marketing to freelancing and remote work, content creation, social media marketing, and investments – there's a suitable method for every taste and preference. The beauty of it is that you don't need any special prior knowledge or technical skills to start making money online. With the right guidance and some commitment, you can find your path to financial freedom and flexibility.

In the upcoming chapters, we'll examine every aspect of earning money online in detail. We'll explain the fundamentals comprehensively, provide practical tips, and present inspiring case studies of successful online earners. Additionally, we'll address the challenges, risks, and data privacy in the online realm to give you a comprehensive understanding of the opportunities for earning money online.

I invite you to step out of your comfort zone and be open to new ideas and possibilities. Earning money online can give you the freedom to determine your own schedule, work from anywhere in the world, and achieve your financial goals. Of course, it requires effort and dedication, but the rewards can be immense.

My aim is for you to find both inspiration and the necessary knowledge through this book to start or expand your online money-making journey. Together, we'll explore the exciting world of earning money online and discover which opportunities suit you best!

I wish you joy and success in reading and implementing the content of this book. May it help you achieve your financial goals and lead a fulfilling life.

Chapter 2: Basics of Making Money Online

Everything You Need to Know at the Beginning

In this chapter, I'll walk you through the fundamental concepts of making money online. Having a solid understanding of these basics is crucial for diving into the world of online earning and maximizing your income.

Making money online offers a variety of options that may seem overwhelming at first. But don't worry, I'll explain everything step by step so that you can easily get started and achieve your personal goals.

One of the most popular methods is called affiliate marketing. As an affiliate partner, you can promote products or services from other companies and earn a commission when someone makes a purchase through your special affiliate link. The beauty of it is that you can earn money by recommending products made or offered by others. It's a win-win situation for everyone involved. To be successful as an affiliate marketer, it's important to find a niche that aligns with your interests and skills and target your audience effectively.

Another way to make money online is by participating in online surveys or completing micro-jobs. Companies offer surveys on specialized platforms to gather opinions and feedback from consumers like you. By taking part in these surveys, you can earn compensation. There are also micro-jobs such as filling out forms, categorizing images, or writing product reviews that you can get paid for online. These small tasks can add up to a substantial income over time.

Freelancing or remote work is another interesting option. If you have specific skills, whether it's graphic design, translation, programming, or writing, you can offer your services online. There are platforms where you can register as a freelancer and find projects. As a freelancer, you work independently and have the freedom to work from anywhere as long as you have an internet connection. Freelancing allows you to utilize your talent and earn money simultaneously. It's important to refine your skills and build a good reputation to be successful as a freelancer.

Content creation and blogging are also popular methods of making money online. If you enjoy writing and want to share your passion with others, you can create your own blog and publish interesting content on a specific topic. By monetizing your blog through advertising, sponsored posts, or selling digital products, you can generate income. Building a successful blog takes perseverance and creativity, but it provides an opportunity to showcase your expertise and connect with your audience.

Another approach is e-commerce and online selling. You can create your own online store and sell physical or digital products. Platforms like Shopify or Etsy offer the means to set up a professional and user-friendly shop. You can either create your own products or source products from other providers and sell them online. Online selling opens up a global customer base and offers significant growth opportunities.

These were just a few examples of the basics of making money online. There are many more options depending on your interests and skills. The key is to explore your passions and figure out which approach suits you best. It's important to take the time to analyze your options and develop a strategy that aligns with your goals.

In addition to traditional methods, there are also creative ways to earn money online. One option is creating and selling digital products such as e-books, online courses, graphic templates, or music. If you have special knowledge or talents, you can package your expertise in digital form and sell it online. Platforms like Amazon Kindle Direct Publishing, Udemy, or Etsy provide the means to make your digital products accessible to a wide audience.

Another possibility is generating passive income by building niche websites or blogs. With proper keyword research and SEO optimization, you can create content that generates organic traffic from search engines. By placing ads or incorporating affiliate links into your content, you can earn passive income as your traffic grows.

Regardless of which method of making money online you choose, building a strong online presence and personal brand image is crucial for your success. By showcasing your personality, expertise, and passions, you can build an engaged community and gain the trust of your target audience.

Utilize social media platforms like Facebook, Instagram, YouTube, or LinkedIn to share your content and connect with your audience. Regularly publish high-quality content that provides value and showcases your expertise. Be authentic and show your personality to build a connection with your followers.

Also, remember to establish professional branding by using an appealing logo, consistent color palette, and a clear message. This will help you stand out and build a strong brand identity.

Building an online presence and personal brand image takes time and continuous effort, but it's an important step to maximize your online earning opportunities.

In the following chapters, I'll provide more detailed information on each method, give you tips to maximize your earnings, and show you how to successfully make money online. The world of online earning offers endless possibilities to achieve your financial independence.

Chapter 3: Affiliate Marketing

Becoming a Partner and Making Money

Affiliate marketing is all about promoting products or services from other companies and earning commissions in return. It's a lucrative way to make money online without having to create your own product or provide customer support. To get started in affiliate marketing, you need to sign up for an affiliate network or a specialized affiliate program.

An affiliate network is a platform that connects affiliates with companies. It offers a variety of products and services that you can promote. Some well-known affiliate networks include Amazon Associates, ShareASale, ClickBank, and CJ Affiliate. These networks make it easier for you to access a wide range of companies and their affiliate programs.

After signing up with an affiliate network, you can choose which products or services you want to promote. It's important to select products that align with your topic or niche and are relevant to your target audience. For example, if you blog about fitness, you could promote fitness equipment, sportswear, or nutritional supplements.

Once you've made your selection, you'll receive special affiliate links or promotional materials that you can place on your website or in your posts. These links are unique to you and contain tracking identifiers to monitor your sales. When a visitor clicks on your affiliate link and makes a purchase, the commission is credited to your affiliate account.

To be successful in affiliate marketing, it's important to create high-quality content and skillfully integrate your affiliate links. Avoid overly promotional posts that might deter your readers. Instead, provide subtle and authentic recommendations that add value to your audience.

It's also helpful to place your affiliate links in various parts of your website or posts. You can incorporate them in product reviews, comparison tables, recommendation lists, or in your resource section. Make sure the links are visible but not intrusive.

Another tip is to focus on products or services that you believe in. If you stand behind the promoted products and have used or tested them yourself, you can make your recommendations more credible. Your audience will trust you more when they sense that you provide honest and authentic reviews.

It's also important to track and analyze your affiliate results. Most affiliate networks offer detailed statistics and reports that show how many clicks, sales, and commissions you generate. Use this information to optimize your strategy. Identify the best-performing products, tailor your content to the needs of your target audience, and improve the effectiveness of your advertising efforts.

Affiliate marketing offers the opportunity for long-term success and generating a stable income. However, it requires perseverance, patience, and continuous work. Building a loyal readership or audience takes time. It's important to consistently deliver high-quality content and engage with your target audience.

Furthermore, you should diversify your affiliate strategy. Don't rely solely on a single affiliate program or income source. Explore different niches, products, and affiliate networks to maximize your chances.

Another way to enhance your success in affiliate marketing is by building relationships with other bloggers or influencers in your niche. You can collaborate, write guest posts, or run joint campaigns to expand your reach and attract new potential customers.

Remember that transparency and honesty are of great importance in affiliate marketing. Disclose to your readers and followers that you use affiliate links to earn commissions. This strengthens trust and credibility within your community.

Chapter 4: Online Surveys and Microjobs

Make Money in Your Spare Time

Welcome to the next chapter of my book, "Easy online money-making explained simply"! In this chapter, we'll explore a flexible and easy method of making money online: online surveys and microjobs. If you enjoy sharing your opinion or completing small tasks to earn extra cash, then this chapter is perfect for you. Let's dive into the world of online surveys and microjobs together.

Online surveys are a popular way to earn money by sharing your opinion on various topics. Companies, market research firms, and organizations are constantly interested in understanding consumer behavior and improving their products or services. Therefore, they are willing to offer money or rewards for participating in surveys.

To earn money with online surveys, you need to sign up for a reputable survey platform. There are many websites and apps that offer surveys, such as Swagbucks, Toluna, Survey Junkie, and many others. Make sure these platforms are legitimate and have a good reputation to ensure fair compensation.

After signing up, you'll need to provide some profile information so that the platform can send you surveys that match your interests. The more information you provide, the more likely you are to receive qualified surveys. Be honest when answering the surveys, as companies are looking for reliable data.

Once you receive qualified surveys, you can answer them in your spare time. The questions may cover various topics, such as your shopping habits, your opinion on products, or your experiences with specific services. Take your time to thoroughly and honestly answer the questions.

For each completed survey, you'll receive compensation in the form of money, gift cards, or other rewards. The compensation varies depending on the survey's length and the company conducting it. Keep in mind that you may need to reach a minimum amount to cash out your earnings.

Online surveys provide a flexible way to earn money as you can answer them in your spare time and from anywhere. However, don't expect to get rich quickly. The rewards can vary, and it may take some time to receive enough surveys to earn a significant amount.

In addition to online surveys, you can also do microjobs to earn money. Microjobs are small tasks or activities for which you can get paid online. These tasks range from simple ones like data entry and research to more creative ones like content writing or graphic design.

There are various platforms that offer microjobs, such as Amazon Mechanical Turk, Fiverr, Upwork, and TaskRabbit. When signing up on these platforms, you can specify the type of tasks you want to do and the skills you have. It's important to clearly and precisely present your skills and experience to attract potential clients.

Once registered on a microjobs platform, you can search for available jobs and apply for them. The nature of the tasks varies greatly depending on the platform and demand. Some examples of microjobs include writing product reviews, translating texts, creating social media posts, or testing websites.

Microjobs provide a flexible way to earn money online as you can choose which tasks to take on. You can adjust your working hours and select the jobs that suit you best or interest you. This allows you to develop your skills and gain new experiences.

To succeed in making money with online surveys and microjobs, here are some tips that can help you: Register on multiple platforms to have a constant selection of surveys and microjobs. Carefully read the requirements before applying. Be reliable and punctual to receive positive ratings. Check reviews and feedback to select reputable jobs.

With online surveys and microjobs, you have the opportunity to make money online in your spare time and supplement your income. Make use of these opportunities to share your opinion, complete small tasks, and receive financial rewards. In the next chapter, we'll explore another exciting method: building your own online shop. Until then, I wish you success with your online earning opportunities!

Chapter 5: Freelancing and Remote Work

Flexible Work from Anywhere

In this chapter, we'll delve into another fascinating way to earn money online: freelancing and remote work. If you dream of being your own boss, working from anywhere, and determining your own working hours, then this chapter is perfect for you. Let's dive into the world of freelancing and remote work together.

Freelancing refers to working independently for various clients and projects. As a freelancer, you are not an employee of a company but offer your services and skills as an independent contractor. This provides you with great flexibility and the opportunity to work for different clients.

The advantages of freelancing are clear. You can set your own working hours, work from anywhere, and offer services that you are passionate about and excel in. As a freelancer, you have the freedom to shape your career in a way that suits you best.

One of the great aspects of working as a freelancer is remote work. Remote work means that you can work from any location as long as you have a stable internet connection. This work style allows you to work from home, cafes, coworking spaces, or even exotic destinations.

The first step to starting as a freelancer is to identify your skills and services. Consider the areas in which you excel and the type of services you can offer. It could be writing, graphic design, web development, translation, social media management, or a variety of other skills.

Once you have identified your skills, it's important to build your online presence. Create an appealing portfolio showcasing your previous work or projects. A well-designed website or a profile on freelancer platforms like Upwork, Freelancer, or Fiverr can help attract potential clients.

Another way to find freelance jobs is by actively applying. Research companies or clients who may need your services and send them a compelling application. Network within your industry to make connections and discover opportunities.

During your work as a freelancer, good communication skills are crucial. Clarify expectations and requirements with your clients, ensure you have all relevant information, and maintain open and transparent communication. This helps avoid misunderstandings and build a good working relationship.

As a freelancer, it's also important to keep track of your financial matters. Set clear prices for your services and ensure you receive fair compensation. Track your working hours and make sure to invoice clients on time. It may also be beneficial to educate yourself on tax considerations and freelancer insurance.

Freelancing and remote work offer you the opportunity to take control of your career and adapt your lifestyle. However, it also requires discipline and self-responsibility to be successful. Be prepared to motivate yourself and manage your time efficiently.

In addition to working as a freelancer, you can also search for remote jobs where you work as a full-time employee for a company but can work from home or another location. More and more companies recognize the benefits of remote work and offer positions in various fields, including customer service, IT, marketing, accounting, and more. Platforms like Remote.co, FlexJobs, and LinkedIn Jobs provide a variety of remote job opportunities.

The trend towards remote work offers you the opportunity to adapt your lifestyle and better balance work and personal life. You can save time and money by avoiding commuting and enjoy the flexibility of structuring your day according to your own needs.

However, there are also challenges in remote work, such as the need for good self-organization, maintaining a clear separation between work and personal life, and overcoming possible feelings of isolation. It's important to develop strategies to stay productive and find a healthy work-life balance.

Chapter 6: Content Creation and Blogging

Creative Writing for Online Success

Welcome to one of the most exciting chapters in our guide to earning money online: content creation and blogging. If you have a passion for writing and enjoy sharing information or telling stories, then this chapter is tailor-made for you. Here, we'll explore the fascinating world of content creation and blogging in detail, showing you how you can achieve online success with your words and creativity.

The term "content creation" refers to creating content in various forms, such as articles, blog posts, videos, podcasts, or social media posts. This content aims to provide information, entertainment, or value to readers, viewers, or listeners. The demand for high-quality and relevant content on the internet has grown enormously in recent years, offering you a fantastic opportunity to leverage your writing skills and earn money online.

Writing a blog is one of the most popular forms of content creation. A blog allows you to publish posts regularly and share your interests, experiences, expertise, or stories with others. There are blogs on nearly every topic, from travel and health to technology. If you have a passion or expertise in a specific area, you can start your own blog and build your audience.

The first step in blogging is to identify your topic or niche. Choose a topic that excites you and about which you have a lot to say. Do you want to write about your culinary adventures, share your travel tips, or share your expertise in a specific field? By bringing in your unique voice and perspective, you can stand out from others and appeal to your audience.

Once you've chosen your topic, it's important to publish high-quality content regularly. Plan your posts in advance and create an editorial calendar to ensure you consistently deliver new content. Be consistent and keep your readers engaged by offering interesting topics, well-researched information, and engaging writing.

An important aspect of blogging is search engine optimization (SEO). SEO involves a set of techniques to optimize your content for search engines like Google and attract more organic traffic to your blog. Research relevant keywords and use them in your titles, headings, and post text. Also, build links to other high-quality websites to improve your credibility and visibility.

In addition to blogging, you can also engage in other forms of content creation. Videos have gained significant popularity in recent years. You can create your own YouTube channel and produce informative or entertaining videos. Podcasts offer another way to utilize your voice and provide interesting content for your listeners. With the variety of formats available, you can reach different target audiences and present your content in different ways.

Success in content creation and blogging requires time, patience, and commitment. It may take some time to build a loyal readership or viewership. Interact with your readers, respond to comments, and build a community around your content. Market your blog or content through social media to increase your reach and attract new readers.

One of the most exciting ways to monetize content creation and blogging is through partnerships and collaborations with companies. You can incorporate paid posts, product reviews, sponsored content, or affiliate marketing. By recommending products or services and earning a commission, you can increase your income. The trust and loyalty of your readers are crucial in this process, so it's important to promote only products or services you believe in and that align with your target audience.

In this chapter, we've provided a comprehensive insight into the exciting world of content creation and blogging. It's an opportunity to leverage your passion for writing to achieve online success. Be creative, authentic, and committed to delighting your readers and building your audience. In the next chapter, we'll explore another exciting opportunity: building your own e-commerce website. Stay tuned and discover the diverse ways to earn money online!

Chapter 7: E-Commerce and Online Selling

Thriving in the Digital Age

Welcome to one of the most exciting chapters in our guide to making money online: E-Commerce and Online Selling. In a world where more and more people are shopping online, building your own e-commerce business is a promising way to succeed and earn money. In this chapter, we'll delve into the fascinating world of electronic commerce and show you in detail how to sell your products or services online.

E-Commerce refers to the buying and selling of goods or services over the internet. It offers companies and individuals the opportunity to make their products accessible to a global audience and reach customers all around the world. With the constant growth of the online market, entrepreneurs have more and more opportunities to bring their business ideas to life and achieve success.

Before diving into e-commerce, it's important to have a solid business idea and know your target audience. Identify a niche or product you want to sell and thoroughly research the market. Analyze the needs and desires of your potential customers and develop a strategy to fulfill them. By focusing on a specific target audience, you can stand out from the competition and build a loyal customer base.

The next step towards online selling success is building your own e-commerce website. There are various platforms and tools available to help you create a professional and user-friendly website. Choose a platform that meets your requirements and offers features such as product listings, shopping carts, payment processing, and shipping management. Design your website to be appealing and user-friendly, gaining the trust of your customers and enhancing their shopping experience.

Another crucial aspect of e-commerce is developing an effective online marketing strategy. To successfully sell your products or services, you need to reach your target audience and make your business known. Utilize different online marketing channels such as search engine marketing (SEM), social media, email marketing, and influencer marketing to promote your products and engage potential customers. Create compelling product descriptions, high-quality images, and videos to capture your customers' attention and motivate them to make a purchase.

Logistics and shipping are also important aspects of e-commerce. Ensure that you can offer efficient and reliable shipping solutions to guarantee customer satisfaction. Collaborate with trustworthy shipping partners and optimize your inventory and warehouse management for smooth operations.

An emerging trend in e-commerce is building your own marketplace. Instead of just selling your own products, you can create a platform where other sellers can offer their products. This allows you to offer a wider range of products and potentially generate more revenue. Manage the marketplace effectively to ensure the quality of the products offered and maintain customer trust.

Additionally, there are other online selling platforms available such as Amazon, eBay, or Etsy. By utilizing these established platforms, you can benefit from their large customer base and trustworthiness. Make use of the tools and features provided by these platforms to showcase your products, receive customer reviews, and optimize your sales.

E-commerce offers a variety of opportunities to make money online. In addition to selling physical products, you can also offer digital products such as e-books, online courses, or software. Furthermore, you can sell services online, such as freelancing or consulting in your field of expertise.

In this chapter, we've provided a comprehensive overview of the exciting world of e-commerce and online selling. It's an exhilarating opportunity to build your own business and achieve online success with your products or services. Be creative, analyze the market, develop a strong online presence, and offer outstanding customer service to maximize your chances of success.

Chapter 8: Social Media Marketing

Captivate Your Online Audience

Welcome to one of the most fascinating chapters of our guide to making money online: Social Media Marketing. In today's digital world, where millions of people are active on social media every day, social media marketing offers a unique opportunity to reach your audience, strengthen your brand, and ultimately make money online. In this chapter, we'll show you how to effectively utilize social media to spread your message, build an engaged community, and achieve your business goals.

Social media has fundamentally changed how people communicate, share information, and do business. Platforms like Facebook, Instagram, Twitter, and LinkedIn provide businesses and individuals with the ability to make their content accessible to a wide audience and establish a strong presence. With the right social media marketing strategy, you can directly target your audience, capture their attention, and build long-term relationships.

The first step in social media marketing is choosing the right platforms for your business. Each platform has its own target audience and style, so it's important to understand which platforms best align with your brand and goals. If you want to share visually appealing content, Instagram might be the right choice. If you want to focus on professional networking, consider LinkedIn. Take the time to analyze your target audience and determine which platforms they are most active on.

Appealing and consistent branding is a crucial aspect of social media marketing. Ensure that your profile picture, header images, and biography reflect your brand's personality. Choose a consistent color palette and fonts to create a professional and recognizable look. Your content should communicate your brand values and provide value to users. Creative and well-designed graphics, photos, and videos will appeal to your target audience and encourage them to share your posts and engage with you.

An effective social media marketing strategy also requires understanding the needs and interests of your target audience. Take the time to thoroughly research your audience and analyze their preferences, habits, and problems. Create content tailored to their needs and provide value to them. Make sure to regularly share relevant and engaging content to maintain the interest and interaction of your followers.

Interaction and engagement are crucial for building an active community. Take the time to respond to comments, answer questions, and provide feedback. Keep conversations going and encourage your followers to share their opinions and experiences. By building a strong bond with your community, you can establish trust and position your brand as a credible authority.

Another important aspect of social media marketing is the use of hashtags. Hashtags help make your posts accessible to a larger audience and increase the visibility of your brand. Use relevant and trending hashtags to maximize your reach and attract potential new followers. But don't overdo the number of hashtags and make sure they align with your content.

To optimize your social media marketing efforts, you can also leverage advertising. Platforms like Facebook and Instagram offer powerful advertising options to target your audience specifically and promote your content. Through targeted ads, you can increase your reach, boost conversions, and direct your audience to specific actions, such as purchasing a product or signing up for a newsletter.

In social media marketing, it's not just about promoting your brand but also building relationships with influencers and other industry experts. Collaborating with influencers can expand your reach and strengthen your credibility. By exchanging content with other industry experts, you can showcase your expertise and expand your network.

Social media marketing offers a wealth of opportunities to make money online. In addition to direct product sales, you can also engage in affiliate marketing partnerships, publish sponsored posts, or monetize your expertise through paid consulting services or training.

Chapter 9: Investing and Trading

Smart and cautious ways to enter the financial markets

In this chapter, we'll delve into the topic of investing and trading. Many people want to grow their money and achieve financial freedom. The financial markets offer various opportunities to accomplish this goal. However, it's important to emphasize that investing and trading come with risks. To be successful, you need knowledge, patience, and a cautious approach.

Before diving into the world of investing and trading, it's important to understand the basic concepts. Familiarize yourself with different types of financial products, such as stocks, bonds, options, futures, and forex. Understand how the markets work and what factors can influence their movements. Learn about fundamental analysis methods to identify market opportunities and make informed decisions.

A fundamental principle in investing and trading is diversification. Spread your investments across different asset classes, industries, and regions to mitigate risk. By doing so, you reduce the risk of losing everything if a particular investment doesn't perform as expected. A balanced portfolio structure helps minimize potential losses and maximize potential gains.

Be cautious and thoughtful when it comes to trading. Financial markets can be volatile and change rapidly. Set clear goals and develop a solid trading strategy. Stick to your strategy and don't let emotions guide you. Take the time to analyze the market before making trading decisions.

Risk management is another crucial aspect of trading. Use stop-loss orders to limit your losses and protect your capital. Employ suitable risk management techniques to control your risk and limit potential losses. Keep an eye on your positions and be ready to close them if market conditions turn against you.

Continuously educate yourself and learn from experienced traders. Attend training sessions, webinars, or seminars to expand your knowledge and discover new trading strategies. Engage with other traders and take advantage of networking opportunities to benefit from their experiences.

There are various types of trading, such as day trading, swing trading, or long-term investing. Find the type of trading that suits you best. Every trader has an individual approach based on their goals and risk tolerance. Find your own trading strategy and continually adapt it to market conditions.

Lastly, it's important to have realistic expectations. The financial market can bring both profits and losses. No trader is capable of consistently generating profits. Be patient and accept that there will be ups and downs. What matters is learning from your experiences and continuously improving your trading skills.

Investing and trading can be exciting and offer financial opportunities. However, remember that they also come with risks. Be cautious, develop solid knowledge, diversify your investments, stick to your strategy, and implement effective risk management. With the right approach and a smart mindset, you can seize the opportunities of the financial market and achieve long-term success.

Chapter 10: Online Courses and Coaching

The Power of Digital Learning and Personal Development

In this extensive chapter, we'll thoroughly explore the topic of online courses and coaching. In today's digital era, diverse opportunities have emerged to share and acquire knowledge online. Whether you want to expand your skills, develop personally, or explore new professional perspectives, online courses and coaching provide a unique chance to achieve your goals. So, let's dive into the world of digital learning and personal development!

Online courses are virtual learning environments where you can engage with a variety of topics and skills. What makes them special is their flexibility: you can access them from anywhere and learn at your own pace. This flexibility allows you to tailor your learning plan to your individual needs and make the most of your time. Whether you want to acquire new professional skills, expand your knowledge, or simply delve deeper into a hobby, online courses offer a wealth of opportunities.

Courses are presented in various formats, including videos, texts, interactive exercises, and presentations. This diverse approach helps you extend your learning to different senses and internalize what you've learned better. Moreover, many online courses provide additional materials and resources to deepen your learning and promote practical application.

One of the greatest strengths of online courses is that they give you access to experts in their field. Many platforms bring together highly qualified professionals and experienced practitioners who want to share their knowledge and experiences. You have the opportunity to learn directly from the best and benefit from their expertise. These experts not only provide well-founded information but can also offer valuable insights and practical advice that you can apply in your personal and professional life.

In addition to online courses, there is also the option of online coaching. Here, you work closely with a coach who helps you define your goals and plan steps to achieve them. Coaching can be applied to various areas, such as career guidance, personal development, health and wellness, or business strategies. The coach will support and motivate you, providing valuable tools and techniques to successfully overcome your individual challenges.

A major advantage of online courses and coaching is the flexibility they offer. You can structure your learning and coaching sessions according to your own needs. This allows you to easily accommodate your professional and personal commitments and create your own individual schedule. This flexibility ensures that you make the most of your learning experience and can track your progress at your own pace.

Furthermore, participating in online courses and coaching provides an opportunity to become part of a dynamic online community. Many platforms offer forums, discussion groups, and social networks where you can engage with like-minded individuals, ask questions, and deepen your knowledge. Interacting with other learners and having the opportunity to share experiences opens up new perspectives and promotes collaborative learning.

Before deciding on an online course or coaching program, it's important to reflect on your goals, interests, and expectations. Consider what knowledge or skills you want to acquire and what kind of support you need. Take the time to research different platforms and read reviews from other participants. Pay attention to the qualifications of course instructors or coaches and make sure they have the expertise and experience to provide you with high-quality learning content and support.

Invest time and energy into your learning experience. Be active, ask questions, take notes, and put what you've learned into practice. Stay motivated and engaged, even when the learning process can be challenging. Make use of the resources offered to expand your knowledge and sharpen your skills. Be open to new perspectives and approach your learning journey with curiosity and enthusiasm.

Online courses and coaching offer you the unique opportunity to develop at your own pace, acquire new skills, and achieve your goals. Utilize these resources to unleash your full potential and drive your personal and professional development. Whether you want to advance your career, pursue a passion, or simply expand your knowledge, online courses and coaching are the key to your success. Dive into the world of digital learning and experience the transformative power of online courses and coaching!

Chapter 11: Cryptocurrencies and Blockchain

The Future of Digital Finance

Welcome to an intriguing chapter on cryptocurrencies and blockchain! In recent years, these terms have gained a lot of attention and disrupted the world of finance. But what exactly lies behind them? How can they influence our lives, and what opportunities do they offer? Let's dive into the world of cryptocurrencies and explore the groundbreaking technology of blockchain.

Cryptocurrencies are digital currencies based on cryptographic principles. One of the most well-known and widely used cryptocurrencies is Bitcoin. However, there are now thousands of different cryptocurrencies, each with its own features and use cases. The key to cryptocurrencies lies in their decentralized nature, which allows transactions to be conducted directly between participants without intermediaries.

The blockchain technology is the backbone of cryptocurrencies. A blockchain is a decentralized and transparent database that records transactions and securely stores information. Each block contains a collection of transactions that are cryptographically linked together, forming a chain of blocks that creates an unalterable record of all transactions. This decentralized nature and the use of cryptographic mechanisms make the blockchain extremely secure and tamper-proof.

The benefits of cryptocurrencies and blockchain are diverse. One major advantage is the transparency and security of transactions. Since all transactions are recorded on the blockchain, they are visible and traceable to all participants. This creates trust and prevents manipulation. Additionally, cryptocurrencies enable fast and cost-effective cross-border transactions without the involvement of banks or other financial intermediaries. This can be especially beneficial for people in developing countries who lack access to traditional financial services.

Another exciting aspect of cryptocurrencies is their potential for financial inclusion. By providing access to financial services for people traditionally excluded by banks, cryptocurrencies can help reduce global financial inequality. People without access to a bank account can receive payments, transfer money, and even take out loans with cryptocurrencies. This opens up new opportunities for economic participation and empowerment.

However, there are also challenges and risks associated with cryptocurrencies. The volatility of prices is a well-known issue that presents both opportunities and risks. The value of cryptocurrencies can fluctuate greatly, leading to substantial gains but also losses. Therefore, it's important to exercise caution when investing in cryptocurrencies and only invest money you are willing to lose. Additionally, the security of cryptocurrencies is a concern as they are an attractive target for hackers. It's crucial to take appropriate security measures to ensure the protection of your cryptocurrencies.

The future of cryptocurrencies and blockchain technology is promising. More and more companies and institutions are recognizing their potential and using them for various applications beyond mere payments. For example, blockchain technology can be used for secure asset transfers, identity management, or conducting voting processes. The use of smart contracts, which automatically execute when certain conditions are met, opens up further possibilities for efficient and transparent business processes.

In conclusion, cryptocurrencies and blockchain technology have the potential to fundamentally change how we think about finance and transactions. They offer opportunities for financial inclusion, secure transactions, and innovative applications beyond traditional finance. However, it's important to be aware of the risks and challenges and make informed decisions. Dive into the world of cryptocurrencies, explore the possibilities, and be ready to participate in the future of digital finance!

Chapter 12: Dropshipping and Amazon FBA

Revolutionary Approaches to Online Selling

Welcome to a fascinating chapter on dropshipping and Amazon FBA! In recent years, these innovative approaches have revolutionized online commerce, allowing entrepreneurs to succeed without significant investments and inventory. Let's dive deeper into the world of dropshipping and learn how to utilize it to build a profitable e-commerce business.

Dropshipping is a business model where you can sell products without holding physical inventory. Here's how it works: you search for suppliers or wholesalers who carry the desired products and are willing to ship them directly to your customers. Instead of storing and shipping the products yourself, you simply forward your customers' orders to the supplier, who then ships the products directly to the customers. This allows you to focus on marketing and sales while leaving the logistical aspects to your suppliers.

The first step in starting a dropshipping business is choosing a suitable niche or product category. It's important to find a market that has demand but isn't overly saturated. Conduct market analysis and research to identify potential trends, target audiences, and competitors. Once you've found your niche, you can search for suitable suppliers who offer those products.

A popular method of conducting dropshipping is by building your own online shop platform. You can use an e-commerce platform like Shopify to set up your online store. Here, you can showcase your products, add product descriptions, images, and prices, and provide your customers with a seamless ordering process. There are also other platforms like WooCommerce, BigCommerce, and Magento that can help you create your online store.

Once your online shop is ready, you can start looking for suppliers. There are various ways to find suppliers, including wholesale directories, online marketplaces, and direct contact with manufacturers. It's important to work with trusted and reliable suppliers to ensure product quality and timely deliveries.

When a customer places an order on your online shop, you simply forward the order to the corresponding supplier. You provide the customer's information and shipping address, and the supplier takes care of the rest of the process. You typically receive a wholesale price for the product while setting the selling price that your customers pay. The difference between the wholesale price and the selling price is your profit.

An important aspect of dropshipping is marketing and customer acquisition. To make your business successful, you need to attract potential customers to your online shop. This is where various marketing strategies come into play, such as search engine optimization (SEO), paid advertising, social media marketing, and influencer marketing. The goal is to drive traffic to your online shop and generate conversions.

Customer service is also crucial to keep in mind. Although you're not directly responsible for shipping and storage, you still carry the responsibility for your customers and their satisfaction. Make sure to answer questions, handle complaints, and maintain clear communication with your customers. Positive customer reviews can drive your business forward and lead to repeat purchases.

In addition to dropshipping, there's another revolutionary method to build a successful online business: Amazon FBA (Fulfillment by Amazon). With Amazon FBA, you send your products to an Amazon warehouse where they are stored, packaged, and shipped. Amazon takes care of the entire logistics, customer service, and even returns processing. This allows you to benefit from Amazon's established infrastructure and trust as the world's largest online marketplace.

With Amazon FBA, you can leverage the reach and credibility of Amazon to make your products accessible to a wide audience. Customers rely on Amazon's fast delivery and excellent customer service, which can give you a competitive advantage. Additionally, you can use the Amazon platform to specifically target potential customers and optimize your product offerings.

It's important to note that both dropshipping and Amazon FBA require thorough research and planning. You need to select the right products, find trustworthy suppliers, optimize your pricing, and develop a solid marketing strategy. It takes time and dedication to build your dropshipping or Amazon FBA business successfully, but with the right approach and determination, you can achieve your goals.

Overall, dropshipping and Amazon FBA offer exciting opportunities to build a successful e-commerce business without significant investments in inventory and shipping infrastructure. By utilizing these approaches, you can focus on what matters most—finding lucrative products, reaching your target audience, and building a strong brand. With creativity, perseverance, and the right strategy, you can carve your own path to online success. Start today and dive into the world of dropshipping and Amazon FBA!

Chapter 13: Online Advertising and Google AdSense

Boost Your Income with Digital Advertising Tactics

Welcome to an engaging chapter on online advertising and Google AdSense! In today's digital era, internet advertising is an essential component for businesses and website owners to increase their reach and generate revenue. Let's dive in and explore the fascinating world of online advertising, specifically the opportunities offered by Google AdSense.

Online advertising encompasses a wide range of tactics aimed at reaching targeted audiences and presenting them with relevant content and offers. Compared to traditional advertising, online advertising offers many advantages, such as targeted placement, measurable results, and broader reach. Companies can tailor their ads to appear specifically to people who are interested in their products or services.

One of the most popular platforms for online advertising is Google AdSense. It is an advertising program by Google that allows website owners to display ads on their websites and get paid for it. The concept behind Google AdSense is relatively simple: as a website owner, you integrate the AdSense code on your website, and Google automatically places relevant ads based on your page's content. When visitors click on those ads or take specific actions, you earn money.

To be successful with Google AdSense, it's important to have high-quality and relevant content on your website. The better your content, the more likely the ads will be relevant to your visitors and encourage them to click. It's also crucial to have a user-friendly website that makes navigation and interaction easy. Good website usability increases the chances of visitors staying longer on your site and potentially clicking on the ads.

Another crucial aspect of Google AdSense is optimizing ad placement. You can experiment with different ad formats and sizes to find what works best for your website and audience. Place the ads in strategic locations that attract visitors' attention, such as near the content or in the sidebar. Skillful ad placement can increase click-through rates and, therefore, boost your earnings.

In addition to Google AdSense, there are other forms of online advertising, such as pay-per-click (PPC) ads, display advertising, video advertising, and social media advertising. Each of these advertising formats has its own benefits and target audiences. If you run a business or own a website, you should test various ad formats and select the ones that align best with your goals.

An important factor to consider in online advertising is the measurability of results. Unlike traditional advertising, online advertising allows you to conduct detailed analytics to see how effective your campaigns are. You can track metrics like click-through rate, conversion rate, and return on investment (ROI) and optimize your advertising strategy based on this data. This enables you to allocate your budget more efficiently and achieve better results.

Another exciting development in online advertising is personalization and retargeting. By using cookies and data analysis, advertisers can personalize their ads and specifically target those who have already shown interest in their products. Retargeting allows you to re-engage potential customers and present them with relevant offers. This increases the chances of conversions and repeat purchases.

However, it's important to keep privacy and data protection in mind when it comes to online advertising. More and more people are concerned about the use of their personal data for advertising purposes. Therefore, it's crucial to be transparent and comply with privacy policies. Make sure to obtain user consent before using their data for advertising purposes and provide them with options to adjust their settings.

Overall, online advertising, especially Google AdSense, offers exciting opportunities to generate income and enhance the success of businesses and website owners. With the right strategy, high-quality content, and targeted ad placement, you can maximize your income and expand your reach. Stay updated on the latest developments in online advertising and continuously adapt your strategy to stay competitive. Harness the power of digital advertising and achieve impressive results!

Chapter 14: Passive Income Strategies

Create Your Financial Freedom

Welcome to an exciting chapter on passive income strategies! In today's fast-paced world, more and more people are looking for ways to generate additional income and achieve financial freedom. Passive income strategies offer an exciting way to do just that. Let's dive deeper into this topic and find out how you can build passive income.

So, what exactly is passive income? Unlike active income, where you have to actively invest time and effort to earn money, passive income allows you to earn money while you sleep. It's a form of income where you continuously generate revenue without constantly working on it. Sounds like a dream, right?

There are various passive income strategies you can consider. Let's explore some of the most popular and effective ones:

Dividend stock investing: A popular strategy is to invest in companies that regularly pay dividends to their shareholders. By purchasing stocks of these companies, you can earn regular income in the form of dividend payments.

Real estate investments: Another proven method to generate passive income is through real estate. You can acquire residential or commercial properties and rent them out. The monthly rental income serves as a stable source of income.

Digital products and online courses: In the digital era, creating and selling digital products and online courses provides a great opportunity to generate passive income. You can create e-books, video courses, audio programs, or other digital content and sell them through various platforms.

Affiliate marketing: With affiliate marketing, you earn money by promoting products or services of other companies and receiving commissions when someone makes a purchase through your unique affiliate link. It requires some initial work, but once you have placed your affiliate links, you can generate passive income when purchases are made.

Automated online businesses: By building an automated online business, you can generate passive income. It could be an e-commerce shop that automatically ships products or a website that earns advertising revenue. With the right strategy and automation, you can generate income without actively working on it.

It's important to note that passive income doesn't mean you don't have to work at all. It often requires an initial investment of time, money, and effort to set up and get passive income strategies running. However, the idea is that these strategies can generate stable income in the long run while requiring less active work from you.

There are some key factors to consider in order to successfully build passive income:

Patience and persistence: Building passive income takes time and perseverance. Be patient and don't give up even if the results aren't immediately visible.

Diversification: Diversify your passive income by investing in different strategies. Don't rely solely on one source of income; build a portfolio of various passive income strategies.

Continuous learning: Stay updated on the latest trends and techniques in the strategies you choose. The world of passive income is constantly evolving, and it's important to stay current to be successful.

Monitoring and adjustment: Regularly monitor your passive income strategies and make adjustments for optimal results. Be open to new opportunities and adapt your strategy to maximize your income.

Remember, passive income is not an instant success. It requires planning, commitment, and continuous effort. However, it's a rewarding journey that can provide long-term financial freedom and flexibility.

In this chapter, you've gained a comprehensive insight into various passive income strategies. Whether you invest in stocks, buy real estate, create digital products, or engage in affiliate marketing, choose one or more strategies that align with your goals and support your financial objectives. Start today and work consistently to build your passive income. The path to financial freedom is in your hands!

Chapter 15: Privacy and Security

Protect Your Online Privacy

Welcome to an extremely important chapter about privacy and security! In our digital world today, where we handle almost every aspect of our lives online, it's crucial to protect our privacy and safeguard ourselves from potential dangers. Let's dive deep into the topic of privacy and security and find out how you can protect your online privacy.

One first step towards ensuring your security is to use strong passwords. Make sure to use unique, complex passwords for each of your online accounts and update them regularly. Avoid simple and easily guessable passwords like "123456" or your name. Remember, passwords are the first line of defense against unauthorized access to your data.

Another important security measure is to enable two-factor authentication (2FA) for your accounts wherever possible. 2FA ensures that, in addition to your password, another form of verification is required, such as a one-time code sent to your mobile phone. This makes it more challenging for potential attackers to access your accounts, even if they know your password.

When browsing the internet, also pay attention to secure connections. Use HTTPS websites, especially when entering sensitive information like credit card details or passwords. Keep your browsers and operating systems up to date to benefit from the latest security updates and patch potential vulnerabilities.

In addition to technical measures, regularly review the privacy settings of your online accounts and social media profiles. Make sure you have control over what information is publicly accessible and who can see your posts. Limit the collection and use of your personal data by third parties by enabling appropriate settings.

Be cautious of suspicious emails, links, or attachments, especially from unknown senders. Phishing attacks are a common method where scammers try to steal your personal data. Never disclose your sensitive information unless you are certain the source is trustworthy. Also, avoid public Wi-Fi networks when conducting confidential transactions, as they can be insecure.

Protecting your home network is also of great importance. Use a secure password for your router and enable encryption. Make sure to regularly update your router's firmware to close security gaps and prevent potential attacks.

Before providing personal data to websites or apps, carefully read their privacy policies. Familiarize yourself with how your data is used, stored, and shared. Look for companies that ensure transparent and responsible handling of your data.

To protect your online identity, you can use a virtual private network (VPN). A VPN encrypts your internet connection and masks your IP address to preserve your privacy and prevent potential surveillance.

Be aware of the risks of social engineering attacks. Be cautious of unknown callers or individuals asking for personal information. Never disclose sensitive data to unfamiliar individuals and be skeptical of unexpected offers or requests.

The security of your personal data and online privacy is of utmost importance. By taking the aforementioned measures, you can minimize your risk and make your online experience safer. Stay vigilant, stay updated on new threats and security practices, and take privacy seriously. Protect your data, protect yourself!

Chapter 16: Success Factors and Mindset

The Key to Success

In this chapter, we're going to dive deep into the factors that contribute to success and the right mindset because they are crucial to being successful in making money online. Your attitude and mindset play a central role in achieving your goals and creating a sustainable income source. Let's delve into the topic and explore how you can strengthen your success factors and develop a positive mindset that leads you to success.

The first step in fostering a successful mindset is to clearly define your goals. Set clear and realistic goals that you want to achieve. By writing down your goals and regularly engaging with them, you gain a clear focus and can concentrate your efforts on the right areas. Visualize how it will feel when you achieve those goals and use that imagination to maintain your motivation.

Another important aspect is developing a positive mindset. Believe in yourself and your abilities to fulfill your dreams and goals. Don't let negative thoughts or self-doubt take over. Use positive affirmations and repeat them regularly to set your subconscious mind for success. Surround yourself with inspiring people who support and encourage you, and avoid negative influences that could hinder your motivation.

Success also requires perseverance and determination. There will be setbacks and challenges, but don't give up. See those obstacles as learning opportunities and chances for personal growth. Don't let failures undermine your motivation; instead, use them as motivation to improve. Learn from your mistakes and adjust your approach accordingly.

A successful mindset also includes a willingness to continuously learn and grow. Be open to new ideas, trends, and technologies. Invest time and energy in your personal and professional development. Read books, attend training, and engage with experts and like-minded individuals. Stay curious and open to change in order to evolve in an ever-changing environment.

An important success factor is the ability to self-motivate. Learn to motivate yourself and maintain your productivity. Identify your personal sources of motivation and consciously use them to drive your goals forward. It could be the freedom to set your own schedule, achieve financial independence, or pursue your passion. Find out what drives you and utilize that motivation to continuously work towards your success.

Having a positive attitude towards change is also crucial. The online money-making market is dynamic and constantly evolving. It's important to adapt and remain flexible. Be willing to try new strategies, adjust your approaches, and learn from mistakes. See changes as opportunities rather than threats. Stay open to innovations and adapt to the changing needs of your target audience.

Lastly, take good care of yourself and prioritize your physical and mental health. A balanced work-life balance is essential for long-term success. Make time for relaxation, exercise, and a balanced diet. A healthy lifestyle supports your energy, concentration, and productivity and contributes to your overall well-being.

Strengthening your success factors and developing a positive mindset are fundamental elements in achieving your goals in making money online. It requires work, dedication, and perseverance, but the rewards can be enormous. Be ready to work on yourself, improve your mindset, and manifest the success you desire. Believe in yourself and your abilities, and let your mindset become your greatest ally. Success is in your hands!

Chapter 17: Success Stories of Online Earners

Inspiration and Success Stories

In this chapter, we'll explore the success stories of online earners. It's inspiring and motivating to hear about people who have managed to make money online and build a successful income. Their stories show us that it's possible to achieve our dreams and attain financial freedom. Let's dive into these fascinating case studies and draw inspiration from their success.

Case Study 1:
Anna - From Hobbyist to Profitable Online Boutique Owner
Anna has always been a passionate crafter. She created beautiful handmade jewelry and initially sold them to friends and family. When she realized the potential of her hobby, she decided to open an online boutique. She created an appealing website, utilized social media platforms to promote her products, and offered excellent customer service. Within a few months, her business started flourishing, and she was able to quit her full-time job. Today, Anna runs a successful online boutique and generates a significant income from selling her handmade jewelry.

Case Study 2:

Max - From Blogger to Author and Mentor

Max had a great passion for travel and began sharing his experiences and tips on a travel blog. His authentic stories and helpful advice quickly attracted a growing readership. Once he had built a loyal community, Max decided to write a book about his travel adventures and self-publish it. The book became a huge success, bringing him not only financial gains but also opening doors for him as a travel mentor. Today, Max hosts seminars and coaching sessions to help aspiring travel bloggers achieve their own success. Through his online business, Max has not only turned his hobby into a career but also helped others fulfill their dreams.

Case Study 3:

David - From YouTuber to Entrepreneur

David has always been a creative mind and loved creating funny videos to share on YouTube. Over time, his subscriber count grew exponentially, and he realized the potential to monetize his talent. He started forming partnerships with brands and placing advertisements in his videos. Additionally, he offered paid premium content and merchandise items for his loyal fans. His YouTube channel evolved into a profitable business, and David established himself as a successful entrepreneur. Today, he has a team of employees who assist him in producing and marketing his content, and he has even developed his own product line.

These case studies show us that it's possible to make money online and build a successful income. However, it requires commitment, creativity, and a willingness to transform our passions and talents into a profitable online business. Each of these successful online earners has their own unique story and path to success. Their stories inspire us to pursue our own dreams and explore the opportunities of making money online.

Whether it's turning a hobby into a profitable business, becoming an expert in a particular field, or building a loyal following through creative content, these case studies demonstrate that there are various paths to online success. Use these stories as a source of inspiration and learn from the experiences of these successful online earners. They can provide valuable insights into how to start, market, and scale your own online business.

Give your dreams a chance and let these case studies motivate you. Be prepared to work hard, grow, and seize new opportunities. With the right mindset, a clear vision, and a willingness to turn your passions into a profitable online business, you too can become a successful online earner.

Chapter 18: Challenges and Risks

On the Road to Success

The journey to earning money online and achieving financial freedom comes with numerous challenges and risks that need to be overcome. However, by being aware of these factors and actively addressing them, we can succeed and navigate around potential obstacles. In this chapter, we will delve into the challenges and risks we may encounter on our path.

One of the biggest challenges is financial uncertainty. Especially in the beginning, generating a stable income can be difficult. It's important to be prepared and have financial reserves to weather any lean periods. A solid financial plan and wise budgeting are essential to alleviate financial pressure.

Another factor we'll encounter is competition. The online market is highly competitive, and regardless of the niche we choose, there are almost always competitors. To stand out and succeed, we need to differentiate ourselves and provide added value. Thorough market research and positioning are crucial to secure our place in the online world.

Moreover, technical challenges pose a hurdle. Running an online business requires certain technical knowledge and skills. We may need to create a website, utilize e-commerce platforms, or be familiar with digital tools and software. Lack of technical expertise can be a barrier. It's advisable to acquaint ourselves with the basics or seek professional assistance.

Time management is another aspect we need to consider. Effective time management is crucial when earning money online. We must be able to allocate our time efficiently and prioritize tasks. Since online ventures often involve a lot of self-responsibility, balancing work and personal life can be challenging. The ability to organize oneself and develop productive work systems is of great importance.

Acquiring customers and marketing our online business can also be challenging. We need to identify our target audience and employ effective marketing strategies. This requires an understanding of online advertising, social media marketing, and search engine optimization. Continuous customer acquisition is vital for scaling our business and achieving long-term success.

Furthermore, we must not overlook technological advancements. The online world is fast-paced and characterized by constant technological changes. To stay competitive, we need to stay informed about new trends and innovations. Adaptability to new technologies is crucial for success in the online business realm.

In addition to the mentioned challenges, there are certain risks we need to consider. One important aspect is the legal and regulatory side. Depending on the nature of our online business, different laws and regulations may apply, such as those related to data privacy, copyright, or consumer protection. We must educate ourselves about the legal requirements and ensure that we operate our online business in compliance with applicable regulations.

Another risk is fraud and security breaches. The online environment carries potential risks of fraud and cybercrime. To protect ourselves, we need to take measures to secure our online activities. This includes safeguarding our personal and financial information as well as utilizing secure payment and transaction methods. A solid online security strategy is of utmost importance to protect our online presence and business.

By being aware of these challenges and risks and proactively responding to them, we can successfully overcome them and shape our path to success. It requires commitment, perseverance, and a willingness to learn from mistakes and continuously develop ourselves. Let's approach the challenges with a positive mindset and use them as opportunities to grow and evolve. Only then can we achieve our goals and unleash our full potential in earning money online.

Chapter 19: Looking Ahead at Future Trends

The Future of Earning Money Online

When we consider the future of earning money online, exciting opportunities and promising trends unfold before us. Technological advancements and ever-changing consumer needs shape the path we will embark on in the coming years. In this chapter, we take a detailed look at future trends and provide insights into how earning money online could further evolve.

Mobile Online Business:
With the ever-increasing prevalence of smartphones and tablets, mobile online business will play an increasingly important role. People use their mobile devices not only for browsing the internet but also for shopping, gathering information, and engaging in social media interactions. This means that companies need to align their online presence and business models with mobile users. Mobile apps, mobile-optimized websites, and personalized mobile experiences will significantly influence future success in earning money online.

Artificial Intelligence (AI) and Machine Learning:
Artificial intelligence and machine learning are becoming increasingly advanced, enabling companies to automate their processes and offer personalized experiences. AI-powered chatbots, for example, can enhance customer service by providing real-time responses to inquiries. Machine learning can be utilized to predict

consumer buying behavior and make personalized product recommendations. The use of AI and machine learning will make earning money online more efficient and customer-centric.

Influencer Marketing and Social Media:
Influencer marketing has evolved into one of the most effective forms of marketing. Influencers have a wide reach and can influence the purchasing decisions of their followers. In the future, companies will increasingly rely on influencers to promote their products and services. Additionally, social media will continue to play a crucial role in earning money online. New platforms and features will enable companies to target their audience specifically and build an engaged community.

Sustainability and Social Engagement:
Consumers are becoming more environmentally conscious and paying increased attention to sustainable products and companies. Awareness of environmental protection and social responsibility will also play an increasingly important role in the online business realm. Companies that integrate sustainability and social engagement into their business practices will gain a competitive advantage and earn the trust of consumers. Sustainability will be a factor not only in products and services themselves but also throughout the value chain and in marketing efforts.

Virtual Reality (VR) and Augmented Reality (AR):
Virtual reality and augmented reality have already made their way into several industries, and their potential in the online domain is enormous. VR and AR provide an interactive and immersive experience that allows consumers to virtually experience products and services before making a purchase. This will revolutionize the online shopping experience and provide companies with an opportunity to showcase their products in new and exciting ways.

The future of earning money online promises exciting developments and opportunities. Companies that adapt to these trends early on and act innovatively will be successful. It is up to us to recognize these changes and adjust our business models accordingly. By meeting customer needs, leveraging technologies, and focusing on sustainable and socially responsible practices, we can pave the way for a successful future of earning money online.

Closing Words:

With this book, we have gained a comprehensive insight into the world of earning money online. We have explored various ways to make money on the internet, explaining the most important aspects and strategies in an easy-to-understand manner. From affiliate marketing to content creation, blogging, social media marketing, and online advertising, we have covered numerous exciting topics.

It has become clear that earning money online is not a simple "get-rich-quick" solution. It requires time, commitment, and a continuous willingness to learn. We have learned that success in online business is built on a solid foundation of in-depth knowledge, a clear strategy, and a positive mindset.

We have also considered the challenges and risks associated with earning money online. From competition to legal aspects and security risks, we need to be aware and proactively respond to them. However, these challenges also offer opportunities for growth and development.

The outlook on future trends has shown that the online world is constantly evolving and offering new earning opportunities. Mobile online business, artificial intelligence, influencer marketing, and sustainable practices are just some of the emerging trends we should keep an eye on. By being flexible and innovative, we can benefit from these developments.

In conclusion, I would like to emphasize that the key to success in earning money online lies in our own determination and perseverance. There may be setbacks, but we should not be discouraged. Let's learn from our experiences, constantly improve ourselves, and stay committed to our goals. With the right knowledge, a clear strategy, and a positive mindset, we can fulfill our dreams and build a successful online business.

I hope this book has provided you with valuable insights and inspiration. Use the knowledge you have gained to embark on your own journey of earning money online. Be bold, be innovative, and always remain curious. The possibilities are limitless, and with dedication and persistence, you can achieve your goals.

Thank you for reading this book. I wish you success on your journey of earning money online!

www.ingramcontent.com/pod-product-compliance
Lightning Source LLC
LaVergne TN
LVHW041221050326
832903LV00021B/737